THE
APOCALYPSE

THE APOCALYPSE

Translated by *Willis Barnstone*

A NEW DIRECTIONS

Manufactured in the United States of America.
New Directions books are printed on acid-free paper.
Published simultaneously in Canada by Penguin Books Canada.
First published as a New Directions Bibelot in 2000. This translation
of *The Apocalypse* originally appeared in *To Touch the Sky*, published by
New Directions in 1999.

Library of Congress Cataloging in Publication Data

Bible. N. T. Revelation. English. Barnstone. 2000
     The Apocalypse / John of Patmos ; translated by
Willis Barnstone.
          p. cm.
     "A New Directions bibelot"
     ISBN 0-8112-1446-X (alk. paper)
     I. Barnstone, Willis, 1927-   II. Title.

  BS2823 .B376 2000
  228'.05209—dc21   00-056075

New Directions Books are published for James Laughlin,
by New Directions Publishing Corporation.
80 Eighth Avenue, New York 10011

INTRODUCTION

The Apocalypse, or Revelation, is attributed to John of Ephesos, also known as John of Patmos, and the island of Patmos, is the most probable site where John composed this great work. The author of the Apocalypse was in the past thought to be also the author of the Gospel of John, and Letters of John, but linguistic and historical evidence prove otherwise. The four synoptic gospels are fully an apology for the Roman occupation of Palestine—"Give unto Caesar what is Caesar's"—so much, that the Roman centurion who headed the execution squad becomes the first to declare Yeshua resurrected; as for Pilate, his hands are washed of the crucifixion, although he ordered it. (In the Greek Orthodox church, he is St. Pilate). Clearly, between the writing of the gospels and their papal canonization in 401 C.E., many hands shaped the words and theology. The Apocalypse, on the other hand, was probably composed in early draft at the end of the first century. It was one of many apocalypses and barely made it into the final canon, suggesting reasons why it was less tampered with. This visionary book of the future and of heaven and hell is not only anti-Roman; Rome is Babylon, the Roman soldiers are symbolized as demon monsters of hell, and the beast, whose code name is 666, is wicked Nero Caesar. There was every reason to feel unfriendly toward Rome the oppressor. Under Nero and Domitian, many Christians and Jews were slaughtered.

The Greek word *apokalypsis* means "revelation" as well as "apocalypse". It is known as a genre of revelatory visionary works, narrated by a prophet in the first person, but also it is "apocalyptic," that is, of great disasters and heavenly salvation. The main source of the Apocalypse in the Bible is Daniel, which is the only apocalypse in the Old Testament. The beasts and the surreal dream atmosphere of this late mythical book, recalling a period of oppression during the Babylonian Captivity of the Jews, is a powerful metaphor for early Christian travails

As a single poem then, the Apocalypse is the great epic poetic work of the New Testament. However, it was not always the custom to lineate either the Old Testament Hebrew or the New Testament Greek in verse. If one looks at the mid-century French *La Bible de Jérusalem*, one sees even Old Testament verse passages in the New Testament rendered in prose. It wasn't actually until the British Revised Version (1885) that large sections of the Old Testament—Psalms,

Proverbs, Song of Songs, Job, long passages in Isaiah and the other prophets—were in verse finally rendered. The Apocalypse, like the Book of Job, is an extended poem, as densely poetic as Blake's "Jerusalem," Whitman's *Leaves of Grass*, or Gerard Manley Hopkins' "The Wreck of the Deutschland." Here it is rendered in loose blank verse. The language is richly symbolic, obscure, allusive; the work is highly structured yet, like the Song of Songs, it is a collage of recapitulations. The Apocalypse is a prophecy of doom and salvation. It ends marvelously with a description of the walls and streets burning in the bejewled city of heaven.

—W.B.

THE APOCALYPSE

CHAPTER 1

The Apocalypse of Yeshua the Messiah, which God gave the Messiah that he might show his slaves what must soon happen. And God signified it by sending it through his angel to his slave Yohanan, who bore witness to the word of God and the testimony of Yeshua the Messiah of everything he saw. Blessed is the one who reads and blessed are they who hear the words of this prophecy and who keep what is written in it. For the time is near.

Yohanan said to the seven churches in Asia:
   Grace be with you and peace from one who is,
   and one who was, and one who is to come,
   and from the seven spirits before his throne,
   and from Yeshua the Messiah, faithful
   witness who is the firstborn of the dead
   and is the ruler of the kings of the earth.
   To him who loves us and freed us from our sins
   by his own blood, and who made us a kingdom,
   and made priests labor for the God and father,
   to him glory and dominion forevermore.
                                        Amen.

And in Daniel, yes:

Look he is coming with the clouds and every eye
    will see him,
even they who stabbed him,
and all the tribes of the earth will mourn him.
                                        Amen.

"I am the Alpha and the Omega," says the Lord,
"who is and who was and who is coming,
and who is the Pantocrator."

I Yohanan your brother, who through Yeshua
share with you suffering and kingdom and endurance
was on the island called Patmos for the word
of God and testimony of Yeshua.
I was fixed in the spirit on the Lord's Day
and I heard behind me a great voice like a trumpet
saying: "What you have seen, write in a book
and send it off to the seven churches,
to Ephesos, Smyrna, Pergamon and Thyatira,
to Sardis and Philadelphia and Laodikeia."

And I turned to see the voice speaking to me,
and when I turned I saw seven gold lamps
and in the midst of the lamps was one like
the Son of People clothed in a robe down to his feet,
and girt around his breasts* with a gold belt.

    _____

    * Although the Greek mastois means "breasts," it is commonly
    translated as "chest" or "waist."

His head and his hair were white like white wool
like snow and his eyes like a flame of fire,
his feet like fine bronze as if fired in a furnace
and his voice like the sound of many waters.
And in his right hand he held seven stars
and from his mouth came a sharp two-edged sword
and his face was like the sun shining in its power.
When I saw him I fell at his feet like a dead man
and he placed his right hand on me and he said:
"Don't be afraid. I am the first and last
and the living one, and I have been dead,
and look, I am alive forevermore
and I have the keys of Death and of Hell.
So write what you have seen and what you see
and after this what is about to happen.
The mystery of the seven stars you saw
in my right hand, and seven golden lamps.
Seven stars are angels for the seven churches
and seven golden lamps are the seven churches."

CHAPTER 2

"To the angel of the church in Ephesos write:
'So speaks one holding seven stars in his right hand,
one walking amid the seven gold lamps:
"I know your work and labor and endurance
and that you cannot tolerate bad men.
You have tried those who say they are apostles

and yet are not, and you have found them false.
You have patience and for the sake of my name
you have persevered and not grown weary.
But I blame you for abandoning your first love.
Remember the height from which you have fallen
and repent and return to your first works.
If not, I'll come to you and take your lamp
from its place unless you repent. But you
have this in your favor: You hate the deeds
of the church of Nikolas,* which I also hate.
Who has ears, hear the spirit speaking to
the churches. To the victor I will give food
to eat which comes from the tree of life
and which stands in the paradise of God."'

"To the angel of the church in Smyrna write:
'So speaks he who is the first and the last,
who was dead and came back into life:
"I know your suffering and your poverty,
but you are rich, and I know the blasphemy
of those who say they are Jews and are not
but come out of a synagogue of Satan.
Do not fear what you are about to suffer.
See, the Devil will throw some of you in prison

---

* A sect considered heretical, the Nicolaitans were accused of
compromising with "pagan" idolatry. Nikolas was a proselyte of
Antioch, one of the first seven deacons in the Jerusalem church.

to test you and you will suffer for ten days,
and I will give to you the crown of life.
Who has ears, hear the spirit speaking to
the churches. And the victor won't be harmed
by the second death."'

"To the angel of the church in Pergamon write:
'So speaks one who has the sharp two-edged sword:
"I know where you live, where Satan's throne is,
and you keep my name, even in the days of Antipas
my witness my faithful one, who was killed
among you in the place where Satan lives.
But I have a few things I hold against you,
for there you keep the teachings of Balaam,
who taught Balak to snare the sons of Israel,
to eat food sacrificed to idols and go with whores.
So you also hold to the teachings of Nikolas.
Repent then or soon I will come to you
and battle them with the sword of my mouth.
Who has ears, hear the spirit speaking to
the churches. To the victor I'll give hidden manna
and I will give a white stone, and on the stone
will be written a new name no one knows
except the one who will receive it."'

"To the angel of the church in Thyatira write:
'These are the words of the son of God
whose eyes are like the flame of fire

and whose feet are like burnished bronze.
"I know your works – your love, faith, your service
and endurance – last longer than the first.
But I blame you that you forgive Jezebel,
who calls herself prophet and teaches and tricks
my slaves to go with whores and consume food
sacrificed to idols. And I gave her time
in which to repent, but she would not repent
her harlotry. See, I will cast her on a bed
and will hurl those who copulate with her
into great suffering if they don't repent
of going with her. And I'll kill her children
with death. And all the churches will know
that I am the one who searches their minds
and hearts. And I will give to each of you
according to your works. To the rest of you
in Thyatira who do not hold this teaching,
who have not known the depths of Satan,
I will not lay another weight on you.
But hold to what you have until I come.
To one who conquers and keeps my works
until the end, and as it says in the Songs:

> I will extend power over the nations
> > and will shepherd them with a staff of iron
> > > as pottery is broken.

And as I have received from my father
I will give away the morning star. Who has ears,
hear the spirit speaking to the churches.""

CHAPTER 3

"To the angel of the church in Sardis write:
'These words are from one holding seven spirits
of God and seven stars: "I know your works,
in name you are alive yet you are dead.
Come and awake and strengthen what is left
and which is soon to die, for I have found
your works were not enacted before God.
Remember then the things you have received
and heard, and hold on to it and repent.
If you don't wake I'll come in as a thief
and you won't know what hour I'll come to you.
But you have the names of a few in Sardis
and they have not defiled their garments.
They will walk with me in white because
they're worthy. The victorious like them
will be clothed in white clothing. I will never
obliterate his name from the book of life,
and I will confess his name before my father
and before his angels. Who has ears,
hear the spirit speaking to the churches."'

"To the angel of the church in Philadelphia write:
'These are the words of the saint, the true one,
and as Isaiah says,

    Who holds the key of David,

    who opens and none will close,

who closes and none will open.
"I know your works, look, I have set before you
an open door and no one can shut it,
since you have little strength and kept my word
and you did not deny my name. Look, I give you
those who are from the synagogue of Satan,
who say they are Jews and are not. They lie.
Look, I will make them come and worship
before your feet and know I gave you my love.
Since you have kept my word of patience,
I too will keep you from the hour of trial
about to come upon the entire world
to test the inhabitants of the earth.
I'm coming soon. Hold fast to what you have
so none can take your crown away from you.
The victor I will make a pillar in the temple
of my God, and you will never leave it,
and on you I will write the name of my God
and the name of the city of my God,
the new Yerushalayim descending from
the sky, and will record my own new name.
Who has ears, hear the spirit speaking to
the churches."'

"To the angel of the church in Laodikeia write:
'These are the words of the Amen, the faithful
and true witness, the origin of God's creation:
"I know your works, that you are neither cold

or hot, and since you are lukewarm, not hot
or cold, I will spit you out of my mouth.
Because you say I am rich and prospered
and need nothing, and you do not know
that you are the wretched and the pitiful
and the poor and the blind and the naked,
I counsel you to buy from me a gold
made pure in fire so that you may be rich,
and have white clothes to wear on your body
so the shame of your nakedness not appear,
and salve to rub on your eyes so you can see.
And those I love I rebuke and discipline.
So strive relentlessly and then repent.
Look, I'm standing at the door and knock.
If you can hear my voice, open the door,
and I'll come in to you and eat with you
and you with me. The victor I will ask
to sit with me on my throne as I too
was victorious and sat with my father
on his throne. Who has ears, hear what the spirit
says to the churches."'"

CHAPTER 4

After this I looked, and there a door opened
in the sky, and the voice of the first I heard
was a trumpet speaking with me saying:
"Come up here and I will show you what

must happen after this." At once I was enveloped
in the spirit and saw a throne standing in the sky
and one seated on the throne. The one seated
looked like stone of jasper and carnelian,
and circling the throne a rainbow like an emerald.
And circling the throne were twenty-four thrones
and seated on the thrones were twenty-four elders
clothed in white garments, and on their heads
were gold crowns. From the throne poured out
lightning flashes and voices and booming thunder,
and before the throne were seven lamps of fire
burning, which were the seven spirits of God,
and before the throne a sea of glass like crystal.

And in the middle and around the throne
were four live animals teeming with eyes
in front and in back.* The first was like a lion
and the second animal was like a calf
and the third animal had a human face,
the fourth creature was like a flying eagle.
And each of the live animals had six wings
and were full of eyes around them and inside,
and day and night they never ceased saying:
    Holy, holy, holy,
    Lord God the Pantocrator,

---

   * The description of the four animals or "living creatures" is
derived from Ezekiel 1:5–10. Since Ireneus, these four animals
have been used iconographically for the four evangelists.

the one who was and is

and is to come.

And when the animals gave glory and honor

and thanks to the one seated on the throne

and to the one who lives forevermore.

The twenty-four elders cast their crowns

before the throne, and said:

Our Lord and God,

you are worthy to receive this glory, honor

and power,

for you made all things,

and by your will they were, and were created.

CHAPTER 5

And I saw in the right hand of him sitting

on the throne a scroll written on the inside

and sealed with seven seals on the back.

And I saw a strong angel who cried out

in a great voice, "Who is worthy to open

the book scroll and break its seven seals?"

And no one in the sky or on the earth

or under the earth could open the book

or look at it, and I wept much since no one

was found worthy to open the book

or look at it. And one of the elders said to me,

"Don't weep, see, the lion from the tribe

of Yehuda, the scion of David, has conquered

and will open the book and its seven seals."

I saw, between the throne and the four animals
and elders, a lamb standing as if slaughtered,
with seven horns and seven eyes which are
the seven spirits of God sent all over the earth.
And he came and took it from the right hand
of the one seated on the throne. And when he took
the book the four animals and twenty-four elders
fell before the lamb, each holding a harp and gold
    bowls
filled with incense, which are the prayers of saints.
And they sang a new song, saying:*
    You are worthy to take up the book scroll
        and to open the seals upon it
    since you were slaughtered and by your blood
        you bought people for God†
    from every tribe and language and nation,
        and for our God
    you made them be a kingdom and priests
        and they will reign over the earth.

I looked and heard the voices of many angels

---

* From Psalm 98:1 and Isaiah 42:10, "Sing to the Lord a new
song."

† *Egorasmenoi* means "bought" or "having been bought." The re-
ligious meaning of "redeemed" may be a fair interpretation, but
it remains an explanation rather than the financial metaphor it-
self.

around the throne and animals and the elders,
and they numbered myriads of myriads
and thousands and thousands, saying in a great voice:
> Worthy is the lamb who was slaughtered
> to receive the power and riches
> and wisdom and strength and honor
>> and glory and blessing.

And every creature which is in the sky,
on the earth and under the earth and on the sea,
and everything in these, I heard them saying:
> To the one seated on the throne
>> and to the lamb
> blessings and honor and glory and dominion
>> forevermore.

And the four animals said: "Amen,"
and the elders fell down and worshiped.

CHAPTER 6

And I saw the lamb open one of the seals
and I heard one of the four animals saying
in a voice that seemed like thunder, "Come!"
and I saw, and look, a white horse
and its rider had a bow and was given a crown
and he went out conquering and to conquer.

And when the lamb opened the second seal,
I heard the second animal saying, "Come!"

Another horse of fire red came out.
Its rider was ordered to take peace away
from earth so men might kill each other,
and he was given a great sword.

And when the lamb opened the third seal,
I heard the third animal saying, "Come!"
And I saw, and look, a black horse,
and its rider held a pair of scales in his hand.
And I heard what seemed to be a voice
in the midst of the four animals, saying,
"A measure of wheat for a denarius
and three measures of barley for a denarius,
and do not damage the olive oil with wine."

And when the lamb opened the fourth seal,
I heard the voice of the fourth animal saying,
"Come!" and I saw, and look, a pale green horse,
and the name of his rider was Death, and Hell
was following him. Power was given them
over a quarter of the globe to kill
by sword and by hunger and by death
and by the wild beasts of the earth.

And when the lamb opened the fifth seal,
I saw under the altar the souls of those
who were slaughtered for the word of God
and the testimony which they held.

And they cried out in a great voice saying,
"How long, O absolute ruler, holy and true,
will you wait to judge and avenge our blood
from those who live upon the earth?"
They were each given a white robe and told
to rest a little time until the number was reached
of their fellow slaves, brothers and sisters
who are to be killed as they were killed.

When the lamb opened the sixth seal I looked
and there took place a great earthquake
and the sun became black like sackcloth of hair
and the full moon became like blood,
and the stars of the sky fell to the earth
as the fig tree drops its unripe fruit
shaken by a great wind. And the sky
vanished like a scroll rolling up
and every mountain and island of the earth
was torn up from its place and moved.
And the kings of the earth and the great men
and commanders of thousands and every slave
and the free hid in caves and mountain rocks,
and said to the mountains and rocks, "Fall on us
and hide us from the face of him who is sitting
on the throne and from the anger of the lamb
because the great day of his anger has come,
and before him who has the force to stand?"

CHAPTER 7

After that I saw four angels standing on
the four farthest corners of the earth,
holding back the four winds of the earth
so that no wind might blow upon the earth
or upon the sea or upon any tree.
And I saw another angel going up
the sky from the rising place of the sun,
carrying the seal of the living God,
and he cried in a great voice to the angels
granted power to harm the earth and sea,
"Do not harm the earth or the sea or the trees
until we have marked the slaves of our God
with a seal on their foreheads."

And I heard
the number of those who were marked, a hundred
forty-four thousand were marked from every tribe
of the children of Israel:
From the tribe of Yehuda twelve thousand sealed,
from the tribe of Gad twelve thousand,
from the tribe of Asher twelve thousand,
from the tribe of Naphthali twelve thousand,
from the tribe of Manasseh twelve thousand,
from the tribe of Shimon twelve thousand,
from the tribe of Levi twelve thousand,
from the tribe of Issachar twelve thousand,
from the tribe of Yosef twelve thousand,

from the tribe of Benjamin twelve thousand,
marked with the seal.

After that I looked, and suddenly a multitude
whose number no one could count, from every
nation and tribe and people and tongue,
standing before the throne and before the lamb,
wearing white robes, holding palms in their hands.
And they cried out in a great voice saying:*
　　Salvation to our God who is sitting
　　on the throne and to the lamb.
And all the angels stood around the throne
and around the elders and the four animals,
who fell down before the throne on their faces
and they worshiped God, with these words:
　　Amen, blessing and glory and wisdom
　　and thanksgiving and honor and power
　　and strength to our God forevermore.

　　　　　　　　　　　　　　　　Amen.

Then one of the elders asked me, saying,
"These people who are clothed in robes of white,
do you know who they are, where they are from?"
And I replied to him, "My Lord, *you* know."
And he said to me, "These people came from
great suffering and they have washed their robes

---

* Psalms 8:3.

and whitened them in the blood of the lamb."
So they stand before the throne of God,
and serve him day and night in his temple.
Seated on his throne he'll spread his tent over them.
They'll not be hungry or thirsty anymore,
no sun will fall on them and scorch their skin,
because the lamb in the middle of the throne
will shepherd them and lead them to the springs
of the waters of life, and God will wipe away
every tear from their eyes.

CHAPTER 8

And when the lamb opened the seventh seal,
there was a half hour of silence in the sky.
I saw the seven angels standing before God
and they were given seven trumpets.
And another angel came and stood by the altar,
with a gold censer, and was given much incense
to offer with the prayers of all the saints
on the gold altar which was before the throne.
And coming with the prayers of the saints,
then the smoke of varied incense arose
out of the hand of the angel before God.
And the angel took the censer and filled it
with fire from the altar and threw it down to earth,
and there came thunders and voices and lightning
flashes and earthquake. The seven angels

holding the trumpets prepared to blow them.

The first angel blew the trumpet. There came hail
and fire mingled with blood and it was thrown
to the earth, and a third of the earth burned up,
and a third of the trees burned up and all green grass
  caught fire.

And the second angel blew the trumpet
and something like a great mountain on fire
was cast into the sea. A third of the sea was blood
and a third of the creatures in the sea died,
who had been alive. A third of the ships sank.

And the third angel blew the trumpet.
From the sky a great star fell, a blazing torch,
and the star fell on a third of the rivers
and across the springs of the waters,
and the name of the star is called Wormwood,
and a third of the waters became wormwood
and many people died from the waters
because they were made bitter.

And the fourth angel blew the trumpet
and a third of the sun was struck by it,
and a third of the moon, a third of the stars,
and a third of their light was darkened,
and the day lost a third of its brilliance

and likewise the night.

And I looked and I heard an eagle flying
in mid-sky, crying out in a great voice:
"Despair despair despair" to the inhabitants
of the earth at the blasts of more trumpets
that the three angels were about to blow.

CHAPTER 9

And the fifth angel blew his trumpet
and I saw a star fall out of the sky
and down to the earth, and the star was given
the key to the shaft of the bottomless pit.
He opened the shaft of the bottomless pit
and smoke rose from the shaft like fumes
from a great furnace. And the sun was darkened
and the air was darkened from the smoke
of the shaft. And out of the smoke came locusts
upon the earth, and they were given powers
like the powers of scorpions upon the earth.
They were told not to damage the earth's grass,
or any green thing, or any tree, but only people
who don't wear the seal of God on their foreheads.
They were told not to kill them but to torture them
for five months, and their torture should equal
the scorpion's torture when it strikes a person.
And in such days the people will seek death,

but not find it, and they will desire to die
but death will escape from them.

The locusts looked like horses prepared for war.
On their heads it was like the crowns of gold
and their faces were like the faces of people,
and they had hair like the hair of women,
and the teeth in their jaws resembled lions.
Their breastplates seemed to be made of iron,
and the noise of their wings was like the noise
of many horse chariots galloping into battle.
And they have tails like scorpions and stings,
and in their tails the power to harm people.
They have a king over them who is the angel
of the abyss, whose name in Hebrew is Abaddon
and in Greek he has the name of Apollyon.
The first despair is over. After the first,
look, there are still two more despairs to come.

And the sixth angel blew his trumpet,
and I heard a voice coming from the four horns
of the gold altar standing before God,
telling the sixth angel who held the trumpet:
"Release the four angels who are bound
at the great river Euphrates." The four angels
were freed, prepared for the hour and day
and month and year to kill a third of the people.
And the number of cavalry of their armies

is two hundred million. I heard their number.
And so I saw the horses in the vision
and the riders on them were wearing breastplates
of fire red and hyacinth blue and yellow sulfur
and the heads of horses were like heads of lions
and fire, smoke, and sulfur* came from their mouths.
From these three plagues a third of humankind
was killed by the fire and smoke and sulfur
spewing from their mouths. The power of the horses
resides in their mouths and in their tails
because the tails are like serpents with heads
and with them they do harm.

The rest of the people who had not been killed
in the plagues did not repent of the work
of their hands so they might go on worshiping
the demons and the idols of gold and silver
and bronze and stone and wood, which cannot
see or hear or walk. And they did not repent
of their murders and magic arts or their dirty
copulations or thefts.

CHAPTER 10

I saw another strong angel coming down from
the sky, clothed in cloud, and the rainbow

---

* *Theion* is also translated "brimstone," meaning sulfur.

was on his head, and his face was the sun,
and his feet like pillars of fire. In his hand
he held a little book open. He planted his right foot
on the sea and his left foot on the land
and cried out in a great voice like a roaring lion.
When he cried out, the seven thunders spoke
in their own voices. When the seven thunders spoke,
I was to write, but heard a voice in the sky,
saying, "Seal what the seven thunders have spoken
and do not write them down." Then the angel,
whom I saw standing on the sea and on the earth,
lifted his right hand to the sky and he swore,
by him who is alive forevermore,
who created the sky and what lives in it,
and the sea and what lives in it, and he said
that time will be no more. But in the days
of the sounding of the seventh angel, when he
is about to blow his trumpet, right then
the mystery of God will be fulfilled
as he informed his slaves who were the prophets.

And the voice I heard from the sky again
spoke to me, saying, "Go take the open scroll
in the hand of the angel standing on the sea
and on the earth." And I went to the angel,
telling him to give me the little book.
And he said to me, "Take it and eat it
and it will make your stomach bitter,

but in your mouth it will be like sweet honey."
And I took the book from the angel's hand
and ate it and in my mouth it was as sweet
as honey but it made my stomach bitter.
Then they said to me, "You must prophesy
again about many peoples and their tongues
and about many nations and their kings."

CHAPTER 11

The angel gave me a reed like a staff. He said:
"Stand up and measure the temple of God
and the altar and those who worship there.
But omit the courtyard outside the temple
and do not measure it, since it has been given
to the Gentiles. They will trample the holy city
for forty-two months. I will give power to
two of my witnesses and they will prophesy
for a thousand two hundred days, wearing sackcloth.
These are the two olive trees and the two lamps
that stand before the Lord of the earth.
And if anyone wants to harm them, then fire
comes out of their mouths and eats their enemies;
and if anyone wants to harm them,
in such way that person must be killed.
These have the power to close the sky
so no rain will drench their days of prophesy,
and they have a power over the waters

to turn them into blood and strike the earth
with every plague as often as they want.

And when they finish their testimony,
the beast rising from the bottomless pit
will make war with them and conquer them
and kill them. Their dead bodies will lie
in the square of the great city,* which is called
spiritually Sodom, and Egypt where their Lord
was also crucified. For three days and a half
members of the tribes and tongues and nations
will stare at their corpses and not let them be placed
in graves. And those who dwell on the earth
will be happy over them and be cheerful
and send each other gifts, since these two prophets
tormented those who dwell upon the earth."

But after three days and a half, the breath
of life from God went into them, and they
stood on their feet, and great fear fell upon
those who saw them. They heard a great voice out
of the sky, saying to them, "Come up here."
And they went up into the sky in a cloud.
Their enemies saw them. And in that hour
there was a great earthquake and a tenth of

---

* The great city in Apocalypse is normally Babylon, but also
identified as Rome, Jerusalem, Egypt, and Sodom, all condemned
for crimes against prophets, God's messengers, and Jesus.

the city fell. And in the earthquake were killed
seven thousand of the inhabitants,
and the rest were terrified and gave glory
to the God of the sky. The second despair
is over. Look, the third despair comes soon.

And the seventh angel blew his trumpet
and there were great voices in the sky, saying:
    The kingdom of the world is now the kingdom
       of our Lord and his Messiah,
       and he will reign forevermore.
And the twenty-four elders, sitting on their thrones
before God, fell on their faces and worshiped God,
saying:
    We thank you, Lord God the Pantocrator,
       the one who is and was,
    because you have taken your great power
       and become King.
    The Gentile nations were angry
       and your anger came
    and also the time for judging the dead
       and giving wages to your slaves, the prophets
    and your saints, and to all who fear your name,
       the small and the great,
    and to destroy the destroyers of the earth.

Then the temple of God in the sky was opened
and the ark of his covenant was seen in his temple

and there came lightning flashes and voices
and thunders and an earthquake and great hail.

CHAPTER 12

Then there was a great portent in the sky,
a woman clothed in the sun, and the moon
under her feet, and on her head a crown
of seven stars. In her womb she had a child
and screamed in labor pains, aching to give birth.
And another portent was seen in the sky,
look, a great fire-red dragon with seven heads
and ten horns, and on his heads seven diadems.
His tail dragged a third of the stars of heaven
and hurled them to the earth. The dragon stood
before the woman about to give birth
so when she bore her child he might devour it.
She bore a son, a male, who will shepherd
all nations with a rod of iron,
and her child was snatched away to God
and to his throne. And the woman fled
into the desert where she has a place
made ready by God that they might nourish
her one thousand two hundred sixty days.

And in the sky were Mikhael* and his angels

---

* Hebrew for Michael.

battling with the dragon. The dragon and his angels
fought back, but they were not strong enough.
No longer was there place for them in the sky.
The great dragon, the ancient snake, who is called
Devil and Satan, the deceiver of the whole
inhabited world, was flung down to earth,
and his angels were flung down with him.
And I heard a great voice in the sky, saying,
"Now has come the salvation and the power
and the kingdom of our God and the authority
of his Messiah, for the accuser of our brothers
and sisters has been cast down, and the accuser
abused them day and night before our God.
They defeated him through the blood of the lamb
and by the word to which they testified
and did not cling to life while facing death.
Be happy, skies, and those who set their tents
on you. Earth and sky, you will know grief,
because the Devil has come down to you
in great rage, knowing he has little time."

When the dragon saw that he had been cast
down on the earth, he pursued the woman
who had borne the male child. And she was given
two wings of the great eagle that she might fly
into the desert to her place where she is nourished
for a time, two times, and half a time away
from the face of the snake. But from his mouth

the snake cast water, a flood behind the woman,
so he might sweep her away on the river.
But the earth helped the woman, and the earth
opened its mouth and swallowed the river
which the dragon had cast out of his mouth.
The dragon was angry at the woman and left
to battle against her remaining seed,
those who keep the commandments of God
and keep the testimony of Yeshua.

Then the dragon stood on the sand of the sea.

CHAPTER 13

Then I saw a beast coming up from the sea,
with ten horns and seven heads and on his horns
ten diadems, and on his heads were the names
of blasphemy. The beast I saw was like a leopard,
his feet like a bear and his mouth like the mouth
of a lion. And the dragon gave him his power
and his throne and fierce power of dominion.
One of his heads seemed to be stricken to death
but the wound causing his death was healed
and the whole world marveled after the beast.
They worshiped the dragon since he had given
dominion to the beast, and they worshiped the beast,
saying, "Who is like the beast and can battle him?"
He was given a mouth to speak great things

and blasphemies. And he was given dominion
to act for forty-two months. Then he opened
his mouth to utter blasphemies against God,
blaspheming his name and his tenting place,
and those who have set their tent in the sky.
He was given powers to battle the saints
and to overcome them, and was given powers
over every tribe and people and tongue and nation.
All who dwell on the earth will worship him,
each one whose name has not been written since
the foundation of the world in the book of life
of the slaughtered lamb. Who has an ear, hear
Jeremiah:

> He who leads into captivity goes into captivity.
> He who kills with the sword will be killed
> by the sword.*

Such is the endurance and faith of the saints.

Then I saw another beast rising from the earth
and he had two horns like a lamb and he spoke
like a dragon. He exercises all the dominion
of the first beast before him, and makes the earth
and its inhabitants worship the first beast,
whose wound of death was healed. He does great
portents,
even making a fire plunge from the sky

---

* Jeremiah 15:2, 14:11.

down to the earth in the sight of the people.
He fools the inhabitants on the earth
by means of the portents he contrives to make
on behalf of the beast, creating an image
to show the beast as wounded by the sword
yet coming out alive. And he had the power
to give breath* to the image of the beast
and the image of the beast could even speak
and cause all who would not worship the beast
to be killed. He causes all, the small and great,
the rich and poor, the free and the slaves,
to be marked on the hand and the forehead
so that no one can buy or sell without the mark,
the name of the beast or number of his name.
Here is wisdom. Who has a mind, calculate
the number of the beast, which is the number
for a human. And the number is 666.

CHAPTER 14

Then I looked, and see, the lamb standing on
Mount Zion and with him one hundred forty-four
thousand who had his name and the name of
his father written on their foreheads. And
I heard a voice out of the sky like the voice
of many waters, like the voice of great thunder,

---

* *Pneuma* means "breath" or "spirit" or sometimes both.

and the voice I heard was like the voice of harpists
playing on their harps. They sing a new song
before the throne and before the four animals
and the elders, and no one could learn the song
except the hundred and forty-four thousand
who have been bought* from the earth. These are
the men who were not defiled by women,
since they are virgins. They follow the lamb
wherever he goes. These were bought from men
as a first fruit for God and the lamb. And in
their mouths no lie was found. They are blameless.

Then I saw another angel flying in midair
with an eternal gospel to proclaim
to those inhabiting the earth and each nation,
and tribe and tongue and people, saying
in a great voice:
>Fear God and give him glory.
>The hour of his judgment is come,
and worship him who made the sky and earth,
>the sea and the springs of water.

Another angel, a second, followed, saying:
>Great Babylon is fallen, is fallen.
>She made all nations drink her wine of passion
>and her filthy copulations.

---

* See note, p. 20.

Another angel, a third, followed them, saying
in a great voice, "All those who worship the beast
and his image and receive a mark on the forehead
or on the hand, even those humans will drink
the wine of the wrath of God, which is poured
undiluted into the cup of the anger
of their God, and they will be tormented
in fire and in sulfur before the holy angels
and before the lamb. The smoke of their torment
will rise forevermore, and there's no rest
day and night for any who worship the beast
and his image or wear the mark of his name.
Such is the endurance of the saints, who keep
the commandments of God and faith in Yeshua.

And I heard a voice out of the sky, saying,
"Write. Blessed are the dead who from now on
die in the Lord." "Yes," the spirit says, "so they
may rest from their labors. Their works
will follow after them."

Then I looked and there was a white cloud,
and seated on the cloud was one who seemed
to be the Son of People, wearing a gold crown
on his head, and he was carrying in his hand
a sharp sickle. Another angel came out
of the temple, crying in a great voice
to the one sitting on the cloud, "Take out

your sickle and reap, for the hour to reap
has come, because the harvest of the earth
is ripe." And the one sitting on the cloud
swung his sickle on the earth, and reaped the earth.
Another angel came out of his temple
in the sky, and he carried a sharp sickle.
Another angel came out of the altar,
who is in charge of fire, and he called
in a great voice to him with the sharp sickle:
"Thrust in your sharp sickle and gather up
the clusters of the vine upon the earth,
because her grapes are ripe." And the angel
thrust his sickle into the ground and gathered
the vintage from the earth and threw it into
the great winepress of the anger of God.
And the winepress was trodden outside the city
and blood came from the press up to the bridles
of horses for a distance of four thousand furlongs.*

CHAPTER 15

And I saw another great portent in the sky,
great and wonderful, seven angels with seven plagues,
the last ones, since the anger of God is fulfilled
in them. I saw what seemed a sea of glass

---

* The Greek says "1600 stadia." A stade is 606 feet. "Stade" is
commonly translated as "furlong" (220 feet), hence 4000 fur-
longs.

mingled with fire, and victors over the beast
and his image and the number of his name,
standing on the sea of glass, holding harps of God.
They sang the song of Moses the slave of God
and the song of the lamb:

> Great and wonderful are your works,
>> Lord God the Pantocrator.
> Just and true are your ways,
>> O king of nations!
> Who will not fear you, Lord,
>> and glorify your name?
> Because you alone are holy,
>> because all nations come
>> and worship before you,
> because your judgments are revealed.

After this I looked. The temple of the tent*
of testimony was opened in the sky,
and the seven angels with the seven plagues
came out of the temple. They were robed in linen
clean and bright and gold belts girding their breasts.
One of the four animals gave the seven angels
seven gold bowls filled with the anger of God
who lives forevermore. The temple was filled
with smoke from the glory of God and from
his power, and none could enter the temple until
the seven plagues of the seven angels were done.

---

* *Skenes:* "tent" or "pavilion."

CHAPTER 16

Then I heard a great voice out of the temple,
saying to the seven angels, "Go and pour out
the seven bowls of the anger of God
onto the earth." So the first went, and poured
the bowl out onto the earth, and a sore
and painful wound came on those with the mark
of the beast and those worshiping his image.
Then the second poured his bowl on the sea
and it turned into blood like a dead man's,
and every living soul died in the sea.
And the third poured his bowl on the rivers
and springs of waters, and it turned into blood.
I heard the angel of the waters saying:

> You are just, the one who was,
>> the holy one.
> for you have judged these things.
> Because they shed the blood of saints
>> and prophets
> you gave them blood to drink,
>> as they deserve.

And I heard the altar respond:

> Yes, Lord God, the Pantocrator,
> your judgments are true and right.

And the fourth poured his bowl onto the sun
and he was able to burn people with great fire.

And the people were burned in a great blaze
and they blasphemed the name of his God,
who holds dominion over these plagues,
and they failed to repent and give him glory.

And the fifth poured out his bowl on the throne
of the beast, and his kingdom turned dark,
and they chewed their tongues from pain.
They blasphemed the God in the sky because
of their pains and their sores and did not repent
from their works.

And the sixth poured out his bowl on the great river,
the Euphrates, and its water dried up
so as to make ready the way for the kings
from the rising sun.* I saw coming out
of the mouth of the dragon, from the mouth
of the beast, from the mouth of the false prophet
three unclean breaths like frogs. For these are breaths
of demons performing portents that go out
to the kings of the whole inhabited world,
to poise them for the battle of the great day
of God the Pantocrator. Look, I'm coming
like a thief. Blessed is the one who watches
and cares for his clothes so he doesn't walk
about naked and his shame become seen.

---

* *Apo anotoles elio*: "from the rising sun," meaning "the East."

And he brought them together in a place
which is called in Hebrew Har Megiddon.*

The seventh poured out his bowl upon the air,
and a great voice came out of the temple
from the throne, saying: "It happened!" There were
the lightning flashes, voices, and the thunders.
There was an earthquake greater than any since
people inhabited the earth, it was so violent.
The city was sundered into three parts
and the cities of the nations fell. Then Babylon
the great was remembered before God,
who gave her the wine cup of its fury of his wrath.
Every island fled and mountains were not found.
Huge hail, heavy as talents, fell from the sky
upon the people and they blasphemed God
for bringing plague with this enormous hail,
because the plague was exceedingly great.

CHAPTER 17

Then came one of the seven angels who held
the seven bowls and he spoke with me, saying:
"Come, I'll show you the judgment on the great
 whore

---

* *Har Megiddon:* "Mountain of Megiddon." English "Armaged-
don" derives from the Greek version *Harmagedon.*

sitting on the many waters, with whom the kings
of the earth have copulated, and with the wine
of her copulations the dwellers of the earth
have got drunk." He took me off to a desert
in the spirit. I saw a woman sitting
on a scarlet beast who was filled with the names
of blasphemy, with seven heads and ten horns.
The woman was wearing purple and scarlet
and was adorned with gold and precious stones
and pearls. She held a gold cup in her hand,
full of the abominations and filth
of her harlotry. On her forehead a name
    was written:

MYSTERY

BABYLON THE GREAT

THE MOTHER OF THE WHORES

AND THE ABOMINATIONS OF THE EARTH

And I saw the woman drunk on the blood of saints
and from the blood of the witnesses of Yeshua.
I was amazed, looking at her with wonder.
The angel said to me, "Why do you marvel?
I will tell you the mystery of the woman
and the beast with seven heads and ten horns
who carries her. The beast you saw was
and is not and is about to come up out of
the bottomless abyss and go to his perdition.
And the inhabitants of earth will be stunned,

whose names have not been written in the book
of life from the foundation of the world,
when they see the beast that was and is not
and is to come. Here is the mind with wisdom:
the seven heads are seven mountains where
the woman sits on them. They are seven kings.
Five have fallen, one is, the other has not
yet, come, and when he comes, short is the time
he must stay. The beast who was and is not,
he too is the eighth and comes from the seven
and goes to his perdition. The ten horns
you saw are ten kings who did not yet take
a kingdom, but they will have their kingdom
as kings for one hour along with the beast.
These are of one mind and render the power
and dominion to the claws of the beast.
They will make war with the lamb and the lamb
will conquer them, because he is the Lord
of Lords and King of Kings. Those on his side
are the chosen and the called and the faithful."

Then the angel said to me, "The waters you saw
where the whore sits, there are peoples and crowds
and nations and tongues. The ten horns you saw
and the beast, they will all hate the whore
and will make her desolate and naked,
and eat her flesh and will burn her up with fire.

For God put in their hearts to do his will
and act with one mind to give their kingship
until the words of God will be fulfilled.
And the woman you saw is the great city
with dominion over the kings of the earth."

CHAPTER 18

After this I saw another angel coming down
out of the sky and with great authority
and the earth was lighted with his glory.
And he cried out in a powerful voice, saying:
    Fallen fallen is Babylon the great.
    She has become a home for demons
    and a prison of every foul spirit
    and a prison of every foul bird
    and a prison of every foul and
    detested beast, since all the nations
    have drunk the wine of passion
    of her copulation, and the kings
    of the earth have copulated with her,
    and the merchants of the earth
    have grown rich on her lechery.

Then I heard another voice out of the sky, saying:
    Come out of her, my people,
    so you will not join in her sins,

so you won't take on her plagues,
because her sins are piled up
    and reach the sky.
God has remembered her iniquities.
Render to her as she has rendered,
  mix her a double portion
  in the cup she has mixed.
As she glorified in the luxury of the flesh,
give her equal torment and sorrow.
  In her heart she says,
  "I sit, a queen,
  I am not a widow
    and will never know grief."
But soon the plagues will come to her,
death and sorrow and famine,
    and in fire she will burn,
for powerful is the Lord God who has
    judged her.

The kings of the earth, who have copulated
with her and lived in lechery, will weep
and beat themselves over her when they see
the smoke of her burning. Standing far off
because they fear the torment, they say:
  Despair despair is the great city
    Babylon, the strong city,
  for in an hour your judgment came.
The merchants of the earth cry out and mourn

over her, since no one buys their cargo now,
cargo of gold and silver and precious stones
and pearls and fine linen and purple cloth
and silk and scarlet and every cedar wood
and every ivory vessel and every vessel
of precious wood and bronze and iron and marble
and cinnamon and spice and incense and myrrh
and frankincense and wine and olive oil
and fine flour and wheat and cattle and sheep,
and horses and chariots and bodies and souls.

    And the autumn fruit your soul longed for
      has gone from you,
    and all the luxurious and the brilliant
      are lost to you
      and never will be found.

The merchants of these things, who became rich
from her, will stand far off because they fear
her torment, her weeping, and her mourning,
which say:

    Despair, despair is the great city
    who was clothed in fine linen
    and purple cloth and scarlet
    and decorated with gold
    and precious stone and pearl.
    In an hour that wealth was desert.

And all captains and seafarers on the ship
and sailors and all those who work the sea
stood far off. And they threw dust on their heads

and they cried out with tears and groans:
>Despair, despair is the city,
>where all who owned ships on the sea
>grew rich from her prosperity.
>In an hour came only desolation.

Heaven and saints, celebrate her downfall,
and apostles and prophets, for God has judged
against her for you." Then one strong angel
picked up a boulder like a great millstone
and hurled it down into the sea, saying:
>With such violence Babylon will be cast down
>>and will be found no more.
>And the voices of harp players and singers,
>>the pipers and trumpeters
>>will be heard no more in you,
>>and the artisan of any trade
>>will be found no more in you,
>>and the sound of the mill
>>will be heard no more in you,
>>and the light of a lamp
>>will shine no more in you,
>>the voice of the groom and bride
>>will be heard no more in you.
>Your merchants were the great men
>>of the earth
>>and all nations were fooled by
>>your sorcery.
>In her was the blood of prophets

        and saints
     and all who were slaughtered
        on the earth.

CHAPTER 19

After this I heard a great voice in the sky,
like a huge crowd shouting:
    Halleluyah!
    Salvation and glory and honor and power
        to our God.
    True and just are his judgments,
    He judged the great whore
    who has corrupted the earth with her harlotry.
    He avenged the blood of his own slaves
        against her hand.

A second time they said:
    Halleluyah!
    And her smoke ascends forever and ever.

Then the twenty-four elders and four animals
fell down and worshiped God, who was seated
on the throne, and said,

                    Amen Halleluyah.

And a voice came from the throne, saying:
    Praise our God

and all his slaves and those who fear him
  the small and the great.

And I heard the voice of a huge crowd
like the voice of many waters and thunders,
saying:
  Halleluyah.
  Because the Lord God and Pantocrator reigns.
  Let us be happy and exult and give him glory,
  for the wedding of the lamb has come,
    and his bride got ready
  and she had to clothe herself in fine linen
      bright and clean,
  a linen of the good acts of the saints.

The angel said to me, "Write. Blessed are
those called to the supper of the wedding
of the lamb." And the angel said, "These words
are the true words of God." I fell before
his feet to worship him. He said to me,
"You must not do that! I am your fellow slave
and of your brothers and sisters who keep
the testimony of Yeshua. Worship God.
To witness Yeshua is the spirit of prophecy."

I saw the sky open, and look, a white horse
and the rider on him called Faithful and True,
and in the right he judges and makes war.

His eyes are flame of fire, and on his head
many diadems, with names written known
alone by him. And he wore a mantle
dipped in blood and his name is called the word
of God. The armies in the sky followed him
on white horses, clothed in fine linen white
and clean. And from his mouth goes a sharp sword
to smite the nations. He will shepherd them
with a rod of iron. He will trample the winepress
of the fury of the anger of God, the Pantocrator.
He wears on his mantle and on his thigh
a name written, "King of Kings and Lord of Lords."

I saw an angel standing on the sun
and he cried out in a great voice, saying:
"To all the birds flying in the middle air,
Come, gather for the great supper of God
to eat the flesh of kings and flesh of captains
and flesh of strongmen and flesh of horses
and of their riders and flesh of both the free
and slaves and small and great." I saw the beast
and kings of the earth and their armies poised
to make war against the rider on his horse
and against his armies. Then the beast
was captured and with him the false prophet,
who had worked miracles on the beast's behalf
and so deceived those who received the mark
of the beast and those who worshiped the image

of the monster. The two of them were cast alive
into the lake of fire burning with sulfur.
The rest were killed by the sword of the rider
on the horse, the sword that came from his mouth;
and all the flying birds gorged on their flesh.

CHAPTER 20

I saw an angel coming down from the sky.
He was holding a great chain on his hand
and the key of the bottomless pit. He seized
the dragon, the ancient snake, who is the Devil
and Satan; he bound him for a thousand years
and cast him into the bottomless pit
and closed it tight and sealed it over him
so he couldn't fool the nations anymore
until the thousand years should be fulfilled.
After that he must be released a short time.
Then I saw thrones and those who sat on them
were given the power to judge. I saw
the souls of those beheaded for their testimony
to Yeshua and for the word of God
and those who had not worshiped the beast
nor the image of him and did not take
his mark on their forehead and on their hand,
and they came to life and reigned with Yeshua
for a thousand years. The rest of the dead
did not come to life until the thousand years

were over. This is the first resurrection.

Blessed and holy are they who take part
in the first resurrection: on these the second death
has no power. They will become priests of God
and of Yeshua and with him they will reign
a thousand years. And when the thousand years
should be fulfilled, Satan will be released
from his prison and will come out to fool
the nations in the four corners of the earth,
Gog and Magog,* to lead them into battle,
whose number is like the sand of the sea.
Then they climbed up and over the width
of the earth and encircled the encampment
of the saints and their beloved city
but fire came down from the sky and consumed
the attackers. The Devil, who had fooled them,
was cast into the lake of fire and sulfur
where both the beast and the false prophet are
and will be tormented forevermore.

I saw a throne great and white, and sitting
on it was he from whose face fled the earth
and the sky, and no place was found for them.

---

* Ezekiel 38–39. Gog, King of Magog – two names that repre-
sent those nations in league against the Church.

I saw the dead, the great and small. They stood
before the throne and there the books were opened.
Another book was opened, which is the book
of life. The dead were judged according to
their works as they were written in the books.
The sea gave up the dead in it, and Hell
gave up the dead in it, and they were judged,
each one according to their works. And Death
and Hell were cast into the lake of fire.
This is the second death, the lake of fire.
And anyone not written in the book
of life was cast into the lake of fire.

CHAPTER 21

And I saw a new sky and a new earth,
for the first sky and the first earth were gone
and the sea was no more. I saw the holy
city, the new Yerushalayim, coming down
out of the sky from God who prepared her
like a bride adorned for her groom. And then
I heard a great voice from the throne, saying:
"Look, now the tent of God is with the people,
and he will spread his tent over them,
and he God himself will be with them,
and he will wipe away each tear from their eyes
and death will be no more. And grief and crying
and pain will be no more. The past has perished."

And he who sat upon the throne said, "Look,
I made all new." And he said, "Write, because
these words are true and faithful." And he said
to me, "It's done. I am the Alpha and the Omega,
the beginning and the end. And to the thirsty
I will give a gift from the spring of the water
of life. The victor will inherit these things
and I will be his God and he will be
a son. But to the cowards and unbelieving
and abominable and murderers and copulators
and sorcerers and all who are false, their fate
will be the lake burning with fire and sulfur,
which is the second death."

One of the angels came with the seven bowls
full of the seven last plagues, and he spoke
with me, saying, "Come, I will show you the bride,
the wife of the lamb." And he took me away
in spirit onto a mountain great and high,
and showed me the city of holy Yerushalayim
coming down out of the sky from God,
wearing the glory of God, and her radiance
like a precious stone, like a jasper stone
and crystal clear. She has a great and high wall
with twelve gates and at the gates twelve angels,
their names inscribed on them, the twelve tribes
who are the sons and daughters of Israel.
On the east three gates and on the north three gates,

on the south three gates and on the west three gates.
The walls of the city have twelve foundations,
and on them twelve names, the twelve apostles of the
    lamb.
The angel speaking to me had a gold
measuring rod to gauge the city and her gates
and walls. The city lies foursquare, its length
and width the same. He gauged the city with
the reed, twelve thousand furlongs in length,*
her length and width and height the same. He gaged
her wall a hundred forty-four cubits,†
by human measurement the same as angels.'

The wall is built of jasper and the city
clear gold like clear glass. The foundations of
the city are adorned with precious stones,
the first foundation jasper, the second sapphire,
third of agate, fourth of emerald, fifth of onyx,
the sixth carnelian, seventh of chrysolite,
the eighth beryl, ninth of topaz, tenth chrysoprase,
eleventh hyacinth, and the twelfth amethyst.
The twelve gates are twelve pearls, each gate
a single pearl, and the great square in the city
is clear gold like diaphanous glass.
I saw no temple in her, for the temple

---

* About fifteen hundred miles.
† Almost two hundred feet.

is Lord God the Pantocrator and the lamb.
The city has no need of sun or moon
to shine on her, for the glory of God
illumined her and her lamp is the lamb.
The Gentile nations will walk around
through her light, and the kings of the earth
bring glory into her. Her gates will never
be shut by day, and night will not be there.
Her people will bring the glory and honor
of nations into her. But no common thing
will enter her, nor anyone who stoops
to abominations and lies, but only those
written in the book of life of the lamb.

CHAPTER 22

The angel showed me a river of the water
of life shining like crystal and issuing
from the throne of God and of the lamb.
Between the great plaza and the river
and on either side stands the tree of life
with her twelve fruits, yielding a special fruit
for every month, and the leaves of the tree
are for healing the nations. All curses
will no longer exist. The throne of God
and of the lamb will be in the city.
His slaves will serve him and will see his face. His
    name

will be on their foreheads. And night will not
be there and they'll need no light of a lamp
or light of sun, for the Lord God will glow
on them, and they will reign forevermore.

Then he said to me, "These words are faithful
and true, and the Lord God of the spirits of
the prophets sent his angel to show his slaves
those things which soon must take place. Look,
I'm coming quickly. Blessed is the one
who keeps the words of this book's prophecy."

I Yohanan am the one who heard and saw
these things. And when I heard and saw I fell
and worshiped before the feet of the angel
showing me these things. And he said to me,
"You must not do that! I am your fellow slave
and of your brothers the prophets and those
who keep the words of this book. Worship God."
And he tells me, "Do not seal the words
of prophecy of this book. The time is near.
Let the unjust still be unjust, the filthy
still be filthy, the righteous still do right,
and the holy one be holy still. Look,
I'm coming soon, and my reward is with me
to give to each according to your work.
I am the Alpha and the Omega, the first
and the last, the beginning and the end.

Blessed are they who are washing their robes
so they will have the right to the tree of life
and can enter the city through the gates.
Outside will be the dogs and sorcerers
and copulators and murderers and idolaters
and everyone who loves to practice lies.

I Yeshua sent my angel to you
to witness these things to you for the churches.
I am the root and the offspring of David
the bright star of morning. And the spirit
and bride say, 'Come.' Let you who hear say, 'Come.'
Let you who thirst come, and let you who wish
take the water of life, which is a gift."

I give my testimony to all who hear
these words of the prophecy of this book.
If anyone adds to these, then God will add
to them the plagues recorded in this book.
If anyone takes away from the words
of this book's prophecy, God will cut off
their share of the tree of life and the holy
city, those things recorded in this book.
And he who witnesses all these things says,
"Yes, I am coming soon."

                    Amen, come, Lord Yeshua.

May the grace of the Lord Yeshua be with all.

THE NEW DIRECTIONS *Bibelots*